CALVES
CAN BE SO CRUEL

Dear Pammy,
It's not the fair
side, but enjoy
anyways!
♡ -Grace
C.
3/94

CALVES CAN BE SO CRUEL

The Best of Rubes® Cartoons

By

Leigh Rubin

A PLUME BOOK

PLUME
Published by the Penguin Group
Penguin Books USA Inc., 375 Hudson Street,
New York, New York 10014, U.S.A.
Penguin Books Ltd, 27 Wrights Lane,
London W8 5TZ, England
Penguin Books Australia Ltd, Ringwood,
Victoria, Australia
Penguin Books Canada Ltd, 2801 John Street,
Markham, Ontario, Canada L3R 1B4
Penguin Books (N.Z.) Ltd, 182–190 Wairau Road,
Auckland 10, New Zealand

Penguin Books Ltd, Registered Offices:
Harmondsworth, Middlesex, England

First published by Plume, an imprint of New American Library, a division
of Penguin Books USA Inc.

First Printing, October, 1990
10 9 8 7 6 5 4 3 2 1

For Teresa, Jeremy, and Ryan

Special thanks to my brother Paull

"You know, old boy, it's about time we did our part for conservation. So let's save some of this sucker for tomorrow's lunch."

"Alright, already! If it will make you happy, I'll get off at the next exit and get directions!"

"Not much in the way of mail except your human rights newsletter. Want me to read it to you?"

There were no dragons left to slay. They were now an endangered species. There were no fair maidens to rescue. They were now feminists. Chivalry was dead. His suit was a little tight. Arthur had come face to face with a middle ages crisis.

Stone Age drag racing.

She was from Warsaw. He was from Krakow.
Together they fell in love and proved that
opposite Poles attract.

The old gray mare ain't what she used to be.

"...And in conclusion, gentlemen, if we are to survive these uncertain financial times, the safest investment we can make is in ourselves!"

"Now children, I'm sure you're old enough to know the importance of a well-balanced meal."

"There'll be no more afternoon snacks for you, young man. You haven't even so much as put a dent in your dinner!"

At Murray's fine diner they only served fresh homemade soup. At least that's what the label on the can said.

"You were right. This place is a goldmine! Why there must be more mailmen in there than we could possibly attack in a year!"

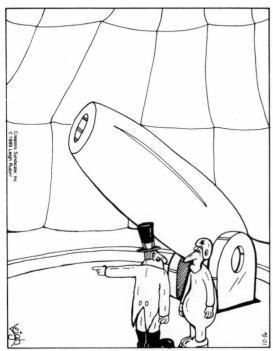

Oddly enough, when the human cannonball's employment was terminated, he wasn't fired.

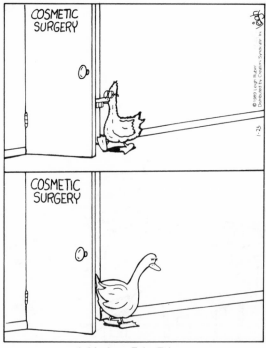

A Modern Fairy Tale

Marcie's shorthand was little more than chicken scratch, her typing hunt and peck at best. She ended up working an unskilled, minimum wage job for an unscrupulous old colonel before her mysterious disappearance.

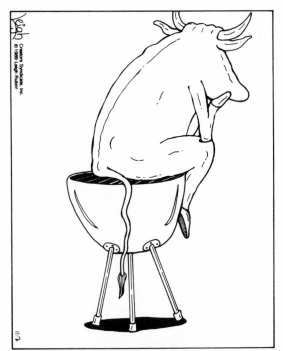

Charged with the matador's murder, the
prime suspect was grilled on the hot seat.
But roasting his rump revealed no beef.
His claim of self-defense wasn't bull.

This little piggy went to market.

Frank wondered if the children could
sense his lack of confidence.

Albert discovers a misnomer.

"Well, if you ask me, the
food here is mediocre at best."

"Rameses! Just what in the name
of Ra are you doing? You're going
straight to your tomb without dinner!"

He had always admired her from a distance,
but never had the courage to break the ice.

X-rayted magazine.

There was no file in the fudge frosted layer cake that Lew's mother sent him in juvenile hall, but he would probably break out anyway.

In a short address to the astonished board, the president tearfully announced the closing of the new underwear division...
To be brief, the board sat in disbelief while their chief, in grief, briefly briefed on the brief briefs.

Marcie spent the last half hour of a
grueling day of house cleaning polishing off
a dusty old bottle of champagne.

I'M SORRY, MR
JOHNSON IS IN A
BEATING. MAY I
TAKE A MESSAGE?

Dungeon secretaries

"Uh, yeah . . . sure, Buddy, I'm off to
see the wizard too . . . hop in the back."

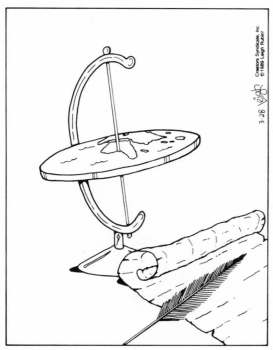

Columbus' first globe.

Petrified Forest

Just in case the water failed
to part, there was always "Plan B."

Onions didn't always agree with Herb.

Nanook's first mistake was flying without enough
fuel. His second . . . kissing the ground after
miraculously surviving the crash.

Diary of a Fish

"Hey, can you believe it's almost spring?
Bet ya gave up on me!"

Where sour cream comes from

Gummy Bears

Ollie, north

Sneezy left the others in pursuit of a solo career and eventually found a lucrative niche endorsing hay fever products.

"Wait a second, old boy. You got lunch
yesterday ... Let me spring for it today."

"... and in this corner,
weighing in at $1.79 a pound ..."

Billy hit a Homer.

"The County Health Inspector is having lunch.
Make sure his plate is extra clean."

After work everybody rushed to "Happy Hour."

Appropriate symbol for the
consequences of Halloween candy.

Although it was bound to ruffle a few feathers,
he would be fried for trying to fly the coop.
Was society to blame, or was he just a rotten egg?

Steamed vegetables.

Milk shake.

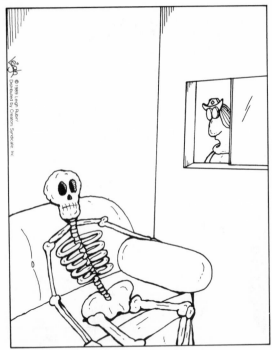

"The doctor will be with you
in just five more minutes."

"Good heavens, Evelyn. These savages
really are uncivilized! They're actually
going to serve us with chablis!"

There was a strange chanting from the barn.
It was true . . . Old MacDonald had a cult.

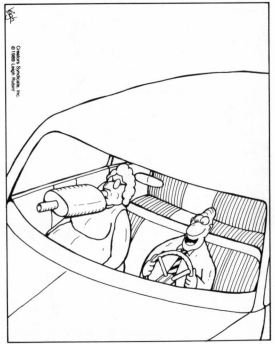

"New muffler really keeps the car quiet, eh honey?"

"As soon as there's an opening we'll be in touch." . . . Sure, that's what they all said. But he knew better. After all, he was nobody's fool.

"What's this world coming to? You can't even eat a worm without worrying that some psycho stuck a hook in it!"

"Did I ever tell you how I got this scar, son? It's from an old college football injury . . ."

He was devastated. It was a John Deere letter.
His tractor of twenty years had left him.

Dorothy turned off the dishwasher.

Gaucho Marx

"Say, didn't your mother teach you that it's not polite for me to talk with your mouth full?"

Herb and Marcy were in
the throws of a messy divorce.

Bull in a china shop.

The light was dim.

The wrinkled prune bought
an old lemon from a bad apple.

The making of cold cuts

Edgar found a loophole.

They had felt the judge's wrath. All hopes of
leniency were crushed. He had put his foot
down and sent the whole sour bunch of them
to the Gallos . . . Ernest and Julio.

It just didn't seem like there was ever a good time to ask for that long overdue raise.

All stared in amazement at the unbelievable
amount consumed during feeding time at the zoo.

In an effort to prevent obstruction of
justice, the aging judge dutifully began
his daily regimen with bran and prune juice.

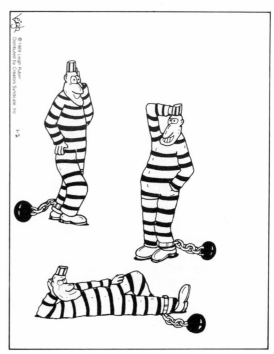

Model prisoners.

Child psychologist

"The anthropology lecture doesn't
begin for an hour. You're early, man."

"Gentlemen, I have reason to believe that there's an imposter among us."

"Well Screaming Eagle, there goes the neighborhood."

It was the little things that occasionally made Marcie suspicious.

Dense Woods

How they make Bacon Bits.

"That reminds me, tomorrow I get the gum."

Despondent over his flash-in-the-pan music career that spawned only one hit single, Frosty ended up destitute, spending the last of his royalties on cheap alcohol that would eventually turn his mind to slush.

"Shame on you, Mr. Johnson! You know the penalty for watching unauthorized programs!"

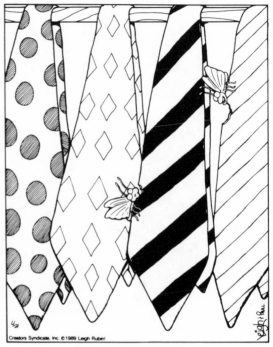

"What did I tell you? . . .
Does this place have terrific tie food or what?!"

"You're right. This polyester
sport coat is absolutely tasteless."

According to statistics, only a small percentage of the millions of packages mailed during the holidays are delayed.

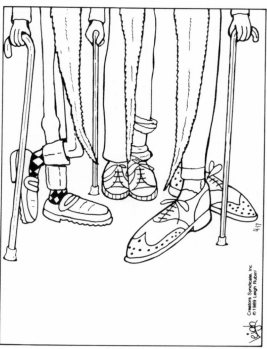

My Three Sons seventy-fifth
anniversary reunion special.

Planned parenthood

"You there! Get up and count those sheep!
And if I catch you falling asleep taking
inventory again, you're fired!"

"Spectacular, Watson! Pinch me so I know I'm not dreaming! We've discovered the legendary temple of the moon god!"

History repeats itself.

"Yesiree, son, that shark put up quite a fight
... of course, so did your grandmother."

"In order to adequately demonstrate just how many ways there are to skin a cat, I'll need a volunteer from the audience."

"Well, it's up to you but
the last one we had tasted funny."

When pressed, the tailor, a material witness in
the suit, came apart at the seams. His altered
testimony completely unraveled. The tale he
had woven had been a complete fabrication.

Aviation Buffs.

Months after the holidays, Nanook would still be eating blubber, lettuce, and tomato sandwiches.

"Gee Pop. When do you think
I'll be old enough to plane?"

"Of course I believe we control our own
destinies. It would be ludicrous to think
that our every action is predetermined."

"Young man, you're not going outside
until you put on at least one coat!"

Woody hid his stage fright well,
despite the knots in his stomach.

The prisoners began to suspect that their fellow conspirator was receiving preferential treatment in exchange for cooperating with the authorities.

"Remember, after we bust outta the zoo, it's important not to attract attention to ourselves . . . so try to maintain a low profile."

"Say old boy . . . care for an after dinner mint?"

"Freeze, you thugs! You're under arrest . . .
Don't move another mussel!"

"Looks like another depressingly wet day as usual."

Predictably, the Annual Morticians' Drag Race
was full of stiff competition.

An unexpected spill turned his
watercolor into an oil painting.

"Listen up, fellas ... I'd like you all to welcome aboard Lenny, our new motivational expert. He's got some interesting techniques to help you increase production."

"Your usual booth, sir?"

"I'm afraid I must be candid with you, Mr. Johnson. According to these test results, you don't have much time left . . . Mr. Johnson?"

Unfortunately, all good things come to an end.

Strip Miner

Although he was a devout believer in Creation, there were times when evolution seemed quite plausible.

At times, Herb and Marcie wondered
whatever possessed them to think
they would enjoy raising a little hell.

Columbus discovers America.

Rocky road

"Your attitude stinks, private! See these stripes? I give the odors around here! You're out-ranked! Get my drift?!"

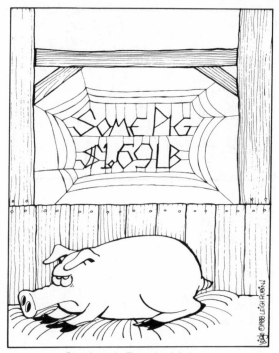

Charlotte's Practical Joke.

"You called *me* a momma's boy?! Why, I've tattled on people for less than that!"

Fire, ignited by a bolt of lightning completely gutted the atheist's meeting hall. Unfortunately for them their insurance policy did not cover acts of God.

A serious head injury occurred at the
Soviet Rhythm Symposium. Or in other words
there was a concussion at the Russian
percussion discussion.

Moses almost blows the job interview.

Billy witnessed the escalating violence.

"Don't get any ideas, Stanley. You know
the doctor told you to avoid saturated fats."

He was understandably apprehensive
about his big date with the princess,
however, the butterflies in his stomach
could be attributed mainly to lunch.

Not surprisingly, he was on the job
only a short time before being canned.

"Here you go . . . It's my famous liver and onions."

"I'll be happy to exchange your defective
boomerang for another one, Sonny . . .
as soon as you bring it back."

Fred had to leave Doris. Their
relationship was going nowhere.

Cannibal Courtship

Overdue books.

"We've, (cough, cough), come a, (hack), long way, (wheeze, cough), babies!"

"Don't stop munching yet . . . we still have one hundred and seventy five box tops to go before we can send away for the rubber raft.

"Yes, Tarzan, you can bring in your
new friend, but for Pete's sake . . .
keep him away from the ceiling fan!"

Out of respect for their deceased
colleague, the rest of the mime
troupe observed a minute of talking.

It had been a long, cramped, dusty,
hot drive. And the wurst was yet to come.

"There's no point losing sleep worrying about
the bills . . . we'll just auction off the kids."

Under constant threat of cattle
rustlers, ranch security was beefed up.

As usual it was just another day
when the boss was on everyone's tail.

The Senior Citizen dating game.